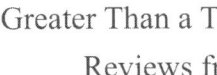

Greater Than a T

Reviews fi

i

Paula Danciu

Aptly titled, you won't just be a tourist after reading this book. You'll be greater than a tourist!

-Alan Warner, Grand Rapids, USA

Thank you for a fantastic book.

-Don, Philadelphia, USA

Even though I only have three days to spend in San Miguel in an upcoming visit, I will use the author's suggestions to guide some of my time there. An easy read - with chapters named to guide me in directions I want to go.

-Robert Catapano, USA

Great insights from a local perspective! Useful information and a very good value!

-Sarah, USA

This series provides an in-depth experience through the eyes of a local. Reading these series will help you to travel the city in with confidence and it'll make your journey a unique one.

-Andrew Teoh, Ipoh, Malaysia

GREATER THAN A TOURIST – TOKYO JAPAN

50 Travel Tips from a Local

Paula Danciu

Paula Danciu

Cover designed by: Ivana Stamenkovic
Cover Image: https://pixabay.com/en/tokyo-kokyo-gaien-skyline-2689771/

Greater Than a Tourist
Visit our website at www.GreaterThanaTourist.com

Lock Haven, PA
All rights reserved.
ISBN: 9781980985136

>TOURIST

50 TRAVEL TIPS FROM A LOCAL

Paula Danciu

BOOK DESCRIPTION

Are you excited about planning your next trip?

Do you want to try something new?

Would you like some guidance from a local?

If you answered yes to any of these questions, then this Greater Than a Tourist book is for you.

Greater Than a Tourist- Tokyo Japan by Paula Danciu offers the inside scoop on Tokyo. Most travel books tell you how to travel like a tourist. Although there is nothing wrong with that, as part of the Greater Than a Tourist series, this book will give you travel tips from someone who has lived at your next travel destination.

In these pages, you will discover advice that will help you throughout your stay. This book will not tell you exact addresses or store hours but instead will give you excitement and knowledge from a local that you may not find in other smaller print travel books.

Travel like a local. Slow down, stay in one place, and get to know the people and the culture. By the time you finish this book, you will be eager and prepared to travel to your next destination.

Paula Danciu

TABLE OF CONTENTS

DEDICATION

This book is dedicated to my family, friends and all the extraordinary people I met throughout my stay in Japan, who brought their own personal magic into my life and made this journey of mine a memorable one.

Paula Danciu

ABOUT THE AUTHOR

After being granted what I believe to be a once-in-a-lifetime job opportunity, I took the leap and moved to Tokyo in 2016 to work as a travel writer with a local company. The Japanese capital welcomed me with open arms and quickly became my second home and I got to spend there some of the best six months of my life.

Nothing sets my heart on fire like traveling and I'm the happiest when able to settle down for a while in a new place and allow myself the time to explore it a slower pace and properly know its culture and people.

Having been fortunate enough to have my beloved passion for a job, I spent my days discovering the best places in Tokyo, learning about the local culture and traditions and eating more noodles in half a year than in my entire life put together.

Despite having already left Japan, a small part of my heart will forever remain in Tokyo. Inspired by my experiences and motivated to share my knowledge

Paula Danciu

and love for this wonderful metropolis, I wrote this book in hopes of helping others plan an unforgettable trip to the Land of the Rising Sun and fall head over heels in love with this phenomenal city, as it happened to me.

HOW TO USE THIS BOOK

The Greater Than a Tourist book series was written by someone who has lived in an area for over three months. The goal of this book is to help travelers either dream or experience different locations by providing opinions from a local. The author has made suggestions based on their own experiences. Please do your own research before traveling to the area in case the suggested places are unavailable.

Paula Danciu

FROM THE PUBLISHER

Traveling can be one of the most important parts of a person's life. The anticipation and memories that you have are some of the best. As a publisher of the Greater Than a Tourist book series, as well as the popular 50 Things to Know book series, we strive to help you learn about new places, spark your imagination, and inspire you. Wherever you are and whatever you do I wish you safe, fun, and inspiring travel.

Lisa Rusczyk Ed. D.
CZYK Publishing

Paula Danciu

OUR STORY

Traveling is a passion of the "Greater than a Tourist" series creator. Lisa studied abroad in college, and for their honeymoon Lisa and her husband toured Europe. During her travels to Malta, an older man tried to give her some advice based on his own experience living on the island since he was a young boy. She was not sure if she should talk to the stranger but was interested in his advice. When traveling to some places she was wary to talk to locals because she was afraid that they weren't being genuine. Through her travels, Lisa learned how much locals had to share with tourists. Lisa created the "Greater Than a Tourist" book series to help connect people with locals. A topic that locals are very passionate about sharing.

Paula Danciu

WELCOME TO
> TOURIST

Paula Danciu

INTRODUCTION

"To my mind, the greatest reward and luxury of travel is to be able to experience everyday things as if for the first time, to be in a position in which almost nothing is so familiar it is taken for granted."
Bill Bryson

Very much like the quote says, Tokyo has an incredible capacity to take the smallest mundane things and make them look extraordinary in the eyes of those uninitiated in the Japanese culture. Ranging from odd to extraordinary, the Japanese capital is a city of contrasts, a place where traditional meets unconventional, where centuries-old traditions live in harmony with the latest technologies and where a strong sense of discipline is matched with a bizarre creativity.

Having a rich culture, fantastic food scene and unlimited choices for entertainment and sightseeing, Tokyo is the city that keeps on giving, one that will astonish you, make you fall in love and leave you longing for a speedy return.

13

Paula Danciu

1. PLAN THE TRIP OF YOUR LIFETIME

Tokyo is one of those cities that are charming all year round with season-specific activities taking place throughout the year, therefore when setting the trip dates it all comes down to your own holiday goals and perhaps climate preferences.

Weather-wise, Tokyo has four seasons, with summer being hot and humid and winter being cold and windy, while temperatures in spring and autumn are milder.

The city's boundless beauty is hard to match and in order to capture nature at its best, consider visiting during the cherry blossom (sakura) season (late-March – mid-April) or during the autumn foliage (koyo) season (mid-October – early-December). Keep in mind that the beginning and duration of both seasons vary every year, so make sure to check the online forecast for the exact dates.

Don't disregard the rest of the year though, as winter comes with gorgeous decorations and summer becomes more enchanting with the fireworks festivals.

2. PRE-DEPARTURE ESSENTIALS

After foolishly forgetting to check the electrical outlet type for Japan prior to my moving there and spending days running around to purchase an adapter, I feel responsible to urge you not to repeat my mistake.If the socket type does not match your country's one, make sure to get an adapter or check with your lodging in Tokyo to see if you can borrow one. With so much to see and do in Tokyo, it's best to be free of any logistic concerns and have your devices charged at all times.

One tool that I found to be a true blessing was Google translator, the image translation function. As a non-Japanese speaker, I found myself staring at labels in the supermarket during my first days in the city. While with some products is easy to guess what they are, with others is not. This app will be a reliable ally in restaurants where English menus are not available or when using a ticket vending machine.

Make sure to download the app at the beginning of your stay and using your phone's camera you'll be able to take pictures of any Japanese text and have it translated into a language you understand. While the translation might not always be 100% accurate, it'll give a clear idea of what you are dealing with.

Tokyo is a gigantic city and is best explored by walking. While trains will take you from point A to B, once you get to an area (whichever that is) you'll have a big amount of walking in front of you, so please make sure to pack your most comfortable pair of shoes to keep your feet free from pain throughout the day.

3. FIGURE OUT HOW TO TACKLE THE CITY

Planning a trip to one of the busiest cities on the planet might seem overwhelming at first. However, once you break the city down into smaller pieces, things suddenly become more manageable. When drafting your sightseeing agenda, I would suggest getting a printed map or using Google maps to gain an overview of what you're dealing with and pinpoint on it all the places that appeal to you.

Having the big image before your eyes will help you observe where are most spots concentrated and give you an idea on how to allocate your time.

Given the grandness of Tokyo, it's best to make smaller divisions based on the hot spots of your choice and stick to one area a day. The use of public transport is unavoidable, however, walking provides the best insight into the urban culture and lifestyle. Tokyo's beauty lies in the small details.

While a minimum of planning is required as with any other trip, I recommend not to overschedule your agenda and allow yourself some flexibility. Tokyo is full of surprises and is likely to stumble upon attractive places that are not included into your itinerary or find some of the spots to be more enthralling than you initially anticipated and want to allocate them more of your time.

In order to avoid prolonged tiredness and power up during the day, I'd suggest you combine various types of activities. Go from a stroll into one of Tokyo' agitated districts to a well-earned rest at an undisturbed garden or spoil your body with a relaxing soak at a public bathhouse before throwing yourself again into the urban fussiness.

4. NAVIGATE YOUR WAY THROUGH TOKYO

Tokyo has one of the most reliable and efficient public transportation networks in the entire world, which makes navigation within the city convenient and facile. Train travel is the most common form of transportation and is likely to cover most of your travel needs. Trains are comfortable, frequent and always on time.

At a first glance, the tangled subway maps can be intimidating and confusing. However, once properly understood, you'll discover a highly-organized system and a well-connected metropolis.

The first important aspect to know is that the railway system is served by multiple operators running both surface and underground trains. Japan Railways is the predominant operator with the most extensive network of train lines running both within the city as well as connecting Tokyo to the rest of Japan. The company also runs the famous Shinkansen, otherwise known as the bullet train.

Paula Danciu

If we think of the Tokyo area alone, we're looking at two companies that serve the underground railway network, namely Tokyo Metro and Toei Subway with a total of 13 lines.

Distinguishing between operators is essential because different railways require separate tickets. The fares are determined by travel distance and tickets can be bought in train stations from vending machines.

Given the huge distances within the city, buying separate tickets for each journey and operator can be pricey and time-consuming. Travel passes, therefore, offer the best deals as they combine operating companies and consistently reduce expenses.

The JR Pass is the most cost-efficient deal for long distance train travel around Japan. If your itinerary includes multiple cities, acquiring the pass will surely pay off. Remember though that since the pass is available for foreign tourists only, it needs to be purchased outside Japan.

However, if your trip is limited to Tokyo, you might find the Tokyo Subway Ticket or the Tokyo Combination Ticket much more suitable.

The first one allows unlimited use of all the 13 lines of the underground and comes in one, two or three-day versions while the second is a one-day pass including besides the underground, all the JR lines within the Tokyo metropolitan area.

The operating hours depend on the company but generally trains run from 4-5 am till sometime around midnight. Tokyo is safe at night so if you happen to miss the last train and you're in close proximity to your accommodation, you can confidently walk back to your place. If not, consider some of my recommended activities for a fun night out, detailed in this guide.

Lastly, you might have seen viral videos circulating on the internet showing station attendants nudging commuters into congested trains to allow the carriage doors to close. Well, those videos are real! I'd advise you to avoid the morning rush hour, which is between 7 and 9 am roughly and either set off for the day really early or wait until the traffic volume relaxes.

5. EXPLORE ONE OF THE WORLD'S STRONGEST CULTURES OF RESPECT

Politeness is one of Japanese society's trademarks and when immersing yourself in a nation with such a solid culture of respect it's a good idea to go prepared.

In Tokyo, locals greet each other by bowing. This goes from a slight nod of the head to a deep bend at the waist. Best time to experience this is when shopping or dining out. You'll feel like royalty as people will serve you with a smile and a bow. My advice is to mirror and match the courtesy. And speaking of restaurants, note that tipping is not customary in Tokyo. Just pay the set price and you're good to go!

Mindfulness of others is strongly rooted in Japanese culture, where instead of only thinking about their own comfort, people live in a constant state of awareness towards their surroundings and others. You'll see proof of this everywhere!

For instance, people in trains will restrain from talking to each other, speaking on the phone or eating as this might inconvenience fellow commuters. When riding an escalator, you'll notice everybody standing on one side and allowing space for those in a hurry to pass by. You'll also spot people walking around wearing surgical masks – this is, in most cases, in order to prevent the passing of illnesses.

Queuing is huge in Tokyo. Expect to queue a fair amount of time during your trip. In fact, never in my life have I seen people more content with having to stay in line as they seem to be in Japan. This sense of order can be observed everywhere and not only in the places you'd expect them, such as restaurants or entrances for different tourist attractions.

Take a simple thing such as boarding a train. The train station platforms will have markings showing where the carriage doors will pull up and you'll quickly notice people lining up behind them, waiting for the train to arrive. No rushing, no stepping in front of the line, simply waiting for one's turn. The same thing can be seen at bus stops.

Locals are usually appreciative of foreigners' attempt to speak their language, hence using some basic Japanese words will go a long way. Two expressions you might want to practice are arigatou gozaimasu (thank you) and sumimasen (excuse me/sorry). While the former can be used at almost every interaction with locals, the latter is going to be terribly useful when navigating crowds (and believe me, there will be plenty of them).

6. TOKYO IS AS CLEAN AS A WHISTLE

Japanese mindfulness and respect go beyond treating others in a polite and thoughtful manner and extends to taking good care and keeping the environment clean by being recycle-conscious and having strict garbage disposal laws in place.

You'll find Tokyo to be one of the cleanest cities you've ever visited even in the most crowded and visited places. Train station bathrooms, regardless of the huge number of daily users are some of the best-maintained facilities I've ever seen in any other place in the world as they're constantly cleaned throughout the day.

While exploring the city, you'll be quick to notice the absence of trash bins. While this can become an inconvenience as at some point it's likely to find yourself in the possession of some form of trash, it's quite admirable how the lack of trash receptacles under no circumstance provides a valid excuse to contaminate the environment. In Tokyo - and all over Japan - people simply don't litter!

When setting off for the day, remember to take a plastic bag with you and use it to collect the waste until reaching a place to dispose of it. Trash bins can be found on train platforms, public toilets and convenience stores. Vending machines also have recycling bins right next to them, however, these are for plastic bottles and cans only.

"Living right in the heart of Tokyo itself is quite like living in the mountains – in the midst of so many people, one hardly sees anyone."
Yūko Tsushima, Of Dogs and Walls

7. ROAM THE STREETS OF TOKYO'S MOST VIBRANT NEIGHBORHOOD

Nothing says "Welcome to Tokyo" better than a meander around the neighborhood that best captures its true essence: the one and only Shibuya.

Shibuya is basically a city within the city, offering everything from culture and shopping to dining and clubbing and is top of my list for all places to be seen in Tokyo. If this is your first time visiting, my best advice would be to go to Shibuya with absolutely no plan and let it inspire you!

Explore the area my way, pop into a convenience store for a can of Chuhai and allow yourself the freedom to roam through the alleys and wallow in the effervescent atmosphere.

Start your journey at the organized chaos that is Shibuya Scramble Crossing. Rumor has it that it's the busiest intersection in the world with hundreds of people sprouting from all directions at the same time when the lights go green. The crossroad is also a favorite spot for New Year's Eve, where thousands of Tokyoites gather for the countdown. If the end of the year catches you around, now you know the best place to be!

8. MINGLE WITH LOCALS AND FELLOW TRAVELERS AT A MEETUP EVENT

There is no better closing to a long day of city rambling than enjoying your favorite drink in the company of like-minded people you can share your travel stories with, and socializing has never been easier thanks to the countless events that are being held on a daily basis throughout the city.

Quickly check out the Meetup website to see which groups you can join and what events are available and get ready to explore the city's party scene. Gatherings of this sort are a hit among foreigners and locals alike.

While there are many organizers out there, my personal favorite community is Welcome Tokyo as they offer a wide range of activities including picnics,

27

language exchanges (perfect chance to enrich your vocabulary with some Japanese phrases), kickboxing, food parties or karaoke and in my experience their events have always been entertaining and were a solid source of awesome people. Usually, there is a small attendance fee charged at the beginning of the event, which includes some light snacks or a drink.

Essential to keep in mind is that these kinds of events have a fixed duration that is most times strictly respected, hence do your best to arrive as early as possible so you don't miss out on all the fun.

Welcome Tokyo also organizes cool trips outside Tokyo so if you're in town for a longer period of time it might be worth checking out their calendar.

9. GO ON A BUDGET SHOPPING SPREE

Despite traveling to one of the world's most expensive cities, don't get discouraged thinking you might not get to do much shopping or spend a fortune on souvenirs.

Japan offers an economical alternative for budget shoppers and a different kind of shopping experience, one that you just cannot get enough of: the 100 yen shop (108 yen, tax included). This concept is the equivalent of the American dollar shop and the stores are spread nationwide and merchandise a wide variety of good quality products ranging from snacks and drinks to cosmetics or interior design items.

Locals regard these shops are reliable sources for household basics, yet in times of souvenir hunting, these are the stores to wander through. Some ideas of Japanese themed souvenirs available here are chopsticks, hand fans, fridge magnets, kitchen towels or sweets.

These shops are everywhere in Tokyo, come in different sizes and belong to different brands. The 3 chains I'd advise you to keep your eyes on are Can Do, Daiso (go to Takeshita Street in Harajuku for the best and largest store) and Seria (gorgeous DIY section).

10. HAVE THE ULTIMATE BATHING EXPERIENCE

Thanks to its plentiful volcanic activity, Japan is home to numerous hot water springs, otherwise known as onsen. Onsen water is rich in minerals and is believed to have curative properties and numerous health benefits especially for the skin.

One superb place worth stopping by is Ooedo-Onsen-Monogatari in Odaiba. The Edo period inspired, lantern-decorated establishment was designed to give the vibe of a summer festival. Shops, restaurants and games are available for entertainment and they also have an outdoor bath (the best kind!) and you'll get to wear a yukata (traditional Japanese attire).

An alternative option to onsen is sento or the indoor public bathhouses. While they might not be as exciting as onsen, they're still a great way to have a relaxing soak after a tiring day. A quick google search on "sento guide" will point you in the direction of the nearest one. Also, make sure to check the opening hours as they might be different between them.

Whichever option you choose to go for, remember that bathing is an important part of Japanese culture and it comes with a well-established set of rules, the two most important ones being that you must shower before entering the pool and that you should be naked, the latter being the one holding back many visitors as the idea of exposing yourself to total strangers might be strange still.

I know I felt that way and for a long time, I was inclined to skip this authentic Japanese experience. But I am glad I didn't! I swear that once you get over the embarrassment, enter the bath and feel the water performing its magic on your body you'll experience a level of relaxation that's hard to match and you will never ever look back!

11. EAT THE BEST SOBA NOODLES IN TOWN

Soba is one of Japan's most popular dishes and one you should make sure to include on your culinary bucket list. Soba is a common choice for lunch or dinner among locals and restaurants are scattered all over Tokyo, however, one in particular, caught my attention and won my heart (or stomach!) forever.

Kiuchi is a tiny authentic Japanese eatery located in Nihonbashiningyocho. Don't be fooled by its modest size, I swear to God this place serves the best soba noodles I found in Tokyo. The food here is mouth-watering and inexpensive with a wide variety of dishes to choose from (both hot and cold) and the service is excellent.

The interior accommodates no more than 10 people at a time plus there's a counter available outside. On sunny days, it's lovely to enjoy an outdoor meal as long as you don't mind standing while eating.

The shop is using the ticket vending machine system so widely spread around Japan. While typically this would be a fast and easy process, brace yourself because the menu here is in Japanese only. If you don't speak the language, this is when google image translate comes in handy! Once you figure out what you're getting, take the ticket and present it to the cook. Your food will be served in just a few short minutes.

12. TREAT YOUR TASTE BUDS TO SOME SWEETS SPECIALTIES

Just a stone's throw away from Kiuchi, on the same side of the street, you'll find one of the best taiyaki shops in Tokyo. Just follow your nose and it will take you to this small gem of a shop that sells terrific fish-shaped waffles filled with either sweetened red bean or sweet potato. Choosing one flavor might be a difficult task, so why not go for one of each?

Any time you feel like having some sugar intake, pop into a convenience store (e.g. Lawson, 7- Eleven or FamilyMart) and get some mitarashi dango, which are tiny balls of mochi (rice cake) skewered on sticks and covered in caramelized soy sauce or daifuku (small round mochi stuffed with various sweet

33

fillings, most commonly the traditional red bean paste).

And if you happen to be passing through Hamacho, make sure to stop by Tokyo Yogashi Club to have a taste of their most popular dessert, the "Mont Blanc". Grab a cup of coffee or tea and savor every bite of this light cake consisting of a mix of fresh cream and custard, wrapped with chestnut paste.

13. HAVE A SPECTACULAR VIEW OVER THE CITY

You haven't truly seen Tokyo or realize its hugeness until you've seen it from above. Tokyo Metropolitan Government Building has become an attractive hot spot for tourists due to its pair of observation decks, located on the 45th floor, one in each of its towers. Access to the observation decks is free of charge which makes this place a far better option than other establishments of its kind, which tend to be quite expensive.

You'll get an exceptional view from 202 meters above the ground over the compact grey city, get to observe the striking contrast between the massive skyscrapers and the average Japanese apartment buildings and spot the green jungle made up of Meiji Jingu and Yoyogi Park. While the view is gorgeous any time of the day, I'd advise you to stop by in the evening as Tokyo looks surreal with the lights on.

14. REVEL IN ONE OF TOKYO'S GREEN OASES

A quick Google search on 'Tokyo' will result in an abundance of photos showing a futuristic yet congested city, jam-packed with impressive grey skyscrapers which seem to leave no room for any greenery.

Having this particular image in my head, I arrived in Tokyo slightly concerned that I might not easily find proper places to take a pause from the noise and bustle of the city. Little did I know that Tokyo excels when it comes to green areas. To me, the Japanese style gardens are the city's best-kept secret.

Often times, tucked away between compact streets and concrete buildings, these gardens are a true haven for locals trying to unwind after a long week at work

35

as well as for tourists looking to take a break from their sightseeing agenda. Many Japanese landscape gardens are designated as sites of exceptional beauty and for good reason.

The moment you set foot in one, the urban fussiness becomes a distant memory. The noise stops and the mind relaxes. Their tranquility lies in the immaculate aesthetics consisting of perfectly groomed lawns and trees which make for a visually satisfying sight.

Some of the best gardens in Tokyo include Rikugien, Hamarikyu, Shinjuku Gyoen or Kiyosumi to name just a few. Each one of these spots has their own charm, however, if you decide to visit more than one you'll notice they all have certain typical elements in common such as a central pond, man-made hills, forested areas and circular walking trails.

The best way to enjoy the experience to the fullest is by wandering around and admiring the garden from different viewpoints. Pay close attention to the ponds as it is common to see koi fish and turtles. When you feel ready for a break, make sure to stop by the teahouse to enjoy a cup of matcha tea while taking in the peaceful vibe and the dazzling scenery.

15. EAT THE FRESHEST SUSHI AT TSUKIJI MARKET

Tsukiji Market, the world's biggest fish and seafood market is a quintessential stop on any visitor's sightseeing itinerary. The market attracts hordes of tourists and is notorious for its 5 am tuna auction. If you're keen on seeing the auction you'll have to get there early to secure a spot as the number of people allowed in to watch the bidding is limited to 120 per day.

Tsukiji is made of an inner market which is the wholesale business area, where the auction takes place and the outer market, that's more tourist-friendly and consists of a maze of narrow lanes lined by many restaurants and shops.

You don't need to wake up before the crack of down to experience the lively and fast-paced vibe of the market. Be there in the morning or around noon and wander through the outer market to gaze upon the broad spectrum of the freshest seafood there is in Tokyo. Go on an empty stomach and have an authentic sushi breakfast or lunch at one of the many eateries serving it, as there's no better spot in Tokyo to indulge in Japan's signature dish rather than its birthplace itself.

If you'd like to take things even further and try your hand at preparing the symbol dish, consider joining a sushi cooking workshop held at Tsukiji and learn from professional chefs the best secrets of making the iconic specialty.

16. CATCH A STUNNING KABUKI SHOW

Just a short stroll from Tsukiji, in Ginza, is Kabukiza, the main theatre in Tokyo to host the famous kabuki performances. Kabuki is a centuries-old Japanese theatre form, known for its dramatic plots, outstanding costumes and elaborate makeup.

Unique about Kabuki is that all roles are performed exclusively by men, the female roles being portrayed by male actors, called onnagata, trained and specialized in the art of imitating women.

Tickets to a full show tend to be costly so if you're a first-timer wanting to satisfy your curiosity or are unwilling to commit to an entire show, single-act tickets, called hitomaku-mi are much reasonably priced. These go on sale on the day of performance and can be purchased directly on the door.

The play itself is something to be remembered. The costumes and masks are dazzling and the action is enthralling and strange in patches. Actors use exaggerated reactions and gestures to convey the complexity of their characters so much so that shows bear a likeness to soap operas. The stories are complemented by live music and an orchestra is most times present, playing traditional Japanese instruments.

The language used is old-fashioned Japanese that even locals sometimes struggle comprehending. In order to fully understand and appreciate what is going on the stage, I'd advise you to rent an English audio guide as having the whole context of the story will most likely enhance your experience.

17. RECHARGE YOUR BATTERIES THE JAPANESE WAY

Touristing around Tokyo can be exhausting. The city is huge, crowded and the list of places to see, countless. But what if I told you that you can take a nap anytime during the day without having to return to your accommodation? All you have to do is catch a train!

Japan makes napping on the train feel more natural and appealing than ever because everyone is doing it. Commuters are doing in on a daily basis and so can you during your trip. Trains are comfortable, safe and everybody keeps quiet (mindfulness of others, remember?). So if you're on a longer ride, don't shy away from closing your eyes and having a rest. No one is going to look at you suspiciously and your belongings will be just fine.

The only risk you're exposing yourself to is not waking up at the right time and missing your stop. However, if you do it long enough, you'll develop this particular talent of regaining consciousness right as the train is reaching your station.

18. HIKE UP A SACRED MOUNTAIN

Remotely located in the south part of the Boso Peninsula in Chiba Prefecture, Mount Nokogiri is a hidden gem many visitors have yet to discover. Besides providing breathtaking panoramic views over Tokyo Bay and Boso Peninsula, the mountain doubles as an important site of spiritual resonance home to Nihonji temple, one of Kanto region's oldest places of worship and to Japan's largest stone Buddha statue.

Easily reachable by train, car or ferry, a day trip to the mountain feels like a breath of fresh air from the hustle and bustle of Tokyo.

To ascend the mountain you can either hike your way up via one of the two main routes or treat yourself to a 5-minute long ropeway ride. The area at the top is connected by a network or walking trails mostly consisting of concrete stairs, some in better condition than others. Whichever option you decide to pick you're looking at a relatively easy hike which can be done at an enjoyable pace.

The walking trails will take you pass countless Buddhist figures and several lookout points. Somewhere along the pathway, sheltered in caves, you'll come across hundreds of small statues (some of them beheaded) depicting arhats or Buddhist disciples who have attained Nirvana and tucked away between high rocks you'll come face to face with the majestic 30-meter tall carving of Hyakushaku Kannon (Goddess of Mercy).

The mountain's most iconic viewpoint is Jigoku Nozoki, aka "a view of hell", which gets its name due to the abrupt valley it overlooks and its fragile-looking shape and serves as a remarkable photo location.

Make sure to pack some healthy lunch and stop by the resting area near the massive statue of Buddha to enjoy your meal while gazing at the serene figure. If possible, stick around until closing time, right before the last ropeway ride to witness a jaw-dropping bright orange sunset.

19. FILL WITH MARVEL AT A MARINE LIFE PARADISE

If you're as much of a marine life enthusiast as I am, then make sure to schedule a day trip to Kamogawa Seaworld in Chiba. This extraordinary establishment is home to over 11,000 sea and river creatures belonging to 800 species and outstanding live performances by killer whales, dolphins, sea lions and belugas are put in place several times per day.

You'll have to be an early bird for this trip and brace yourself for a 2-hour long bus ride to reach your destination. When searching for the best price deal, the GOGO ticket (package including the round-trip bus ticket and admission fare) should do the trick.

I'd advise you to follow the well-established daily program available at the entrance, including the performances and feeding times. This way you won't miss anything! There's plenty to see and do, and trust me when I say that some shows will leave you speechless and you'll want to re-watch (I personally watched the killer whale show three times and yes, it was that good!).

The live performances are stunning! Expect singing dolphins and trainers being thrown up in the air by gigantic whales. It's incredible to see how well directed and perfectly executed the shows are. Some are comical, others impressive, but there's something uniquely entertaining about them all.

Might be a good idea to pack something warmer to wear in the afternoon as the Seaworld is located right on the ocean's coast and the air can get pretty chilly. If you're planning to occupy a front row seat for the killer whale performance, make sure to bring a raincoat. These animals can jump very high despite their massive weight, causing a big splash of water on their way back to the pool.

20. TAKE A WALK OVER THE RAINBOW

The Rainbow Bridge is one of Tokyo's emblematic landmarks which connects Odaiba to the rest of Tokyo.

While most people transfer from one side to the other by car or train, not so many are aware of the pedestrian pathway that goes alongside traffic lanes and is accessible free of charge.

Known as the Rainbow Promenade, a one-way walk takes no longer than 30 minutes and there are two routes you can choose from - the north route offers glittering views over Tokyo skyline and Tokyo Tower while the south route overlooks the Odaiba waterfront. Depending on your start point, the closest stations to the visitor center are Shibaura-futo on the Tokyo side or Odaiba-Kaihinkoen on the Odaiba side.

The views from both sides are gorgeous so there really is no wrong choice. In my experience, Odaiba looks its best in the twilight so if you're thinking to take some great shots of the harbor, I'd suggest crossing the bridge on the south side right before sunset. Choosing the north side for the return journey will leave you in awe as by that time Tokyo's high-rises will be all lit up.

21. WATCH A SPLENDID SUNSET ON AN ICONIC ISLAND

If I had to choose one place in Tokyo to watch the sunset for the rest of my life I would choose Odaiba in the blink of an eye.

The artificial island is a space of exceptional natural beauty with a mix of sandy beaches, green lawns and stunning views over the waterfront, which makes the location to be just perfect for a day outing. Locals choose to chill here especially during weekends and on warm days.

If you feel like taking a break from visiting the busy city, pack some snacks and a blanket for extra comfort and head off to the island for a well-deserved rest. An entire day could be spent simply roaming on the beach, sunbathing and relaxing at Shiokaze Park.

There is no question that the highlight of the day is the breathtaking sunset. As the moment approaches, the place teems with visitors. Watching the sun go to sleep behind the skyscrapers and leaving the sky on fire is such an awe-inspiring sight and one that will stay with you long after your trip ends. Take all the time you need to enjoy the peaceful and refreshing evening air and take in the gorgeous scenery. And don't forget to take some epic photos with the emblematic Rainbow Bridge in the background!

"If your computer speaks English, it was probably made in Japan."

Alan Perlis

22. TAKE A GLIMPSE INTO THE FUTURE

Nothing says Japan like innovation and cutting-edge technology and the place that gathers under one roof the latest technological marvels while making learning exciting and fun is without a doubt Miraikan, Japan's major science center.

The museum addresses areas such as robotics and exploration of space and Earth and besides being substantially informative, what truly sets it apart is all the hands-on experience it provides through quite a number of interactive games and engaging activities. In case you're traveling with kids, this is a good spot to nourish the little ones' love and curiosity for science.

Some of the highlights include the scale model of the international space station showcasing astronauts' living conditions in space and the demonstration show of the humanoid robot ASIMO which is worth the visit alone.

Given its entertaining nature, it's easy to lose track of time and from my experience, about half a day would suffice to deeply explore the exhibition.

Unquestionably, the museum's finest feature is the display of some of the world's most advanced androids and you might be getting goosebumps when seeing the stunning resemblance to humans some of them have. The good news is that each day between certain hours, visitors are allowed to get in contact with and control some of the androids, which makes it amusing (or scary!) to image a world where humans live alongside robots.

If you're interested in learning even more on what the future holds in terms of robotics, make sure to also check the dates for Japan Robot Week and

International Robot Exhibition, two major trade shows held in Tokyo.

23. HAVE A PURIKURA PHOTO SESSION

Purikura are coin-operated photo booths that come with a broad selection of editing options and photos are printed on stickers making them a lovely souvenir to bring back home.

Taking some hilarious photos is a great way to make long-lasting memories and experience a part of the local culture that's highly popular among Japanese teenagers.

When in Shibuya, I'd suggest you stop by Purikura no Mecca, a place whose name does full justice to what awaits inside. This shop is a legit purikura-land. Besides being packed with booths, a costume renting service is available and the outfit collection includes Snow White, French maids or Sailor moon girls. One of the best things about this place is the small studio located at the back which comes decorated with colorful heart-shaped balloons and gigantic teddy bears.

Pick your favorite character, get all dressed up and ready to pose for the camera. You don't have to be a natural born model to have one of the most entertaining photo shootings of your life as this counts as one of those experiences you can only have in Japan.

The studio does not come with a professional photographer so you'll have to either take turns if traveling with a companion or rely on the help of other customers.

Everyone is more than welcome, however, note that this place like many others of its kind requires men to be accompanied by a woman.

24. SING YOUR HEART OUT AT KARAOKE

There are many forms of entertainment in Tokyo and then there's karaoke that beats them all! Karaoke is native to Japan and adored by locals regardless of age or background.

The years of practice and concept development makes Tokyo a singing haven packed with karaoke establishments. I chose to call them establishments because I want you to forget the idea of the typical karaoke bar and picture entire multiple story buildings filled with private karaoke rooms.

As you're passing by these places you're likely to be approached by staff trying to lure you in. Don't resist it! Your singing ability simply does not matter! Whether you consider yourself to be a talented or a lousy singer, there's no scenario in which a night of karaoke could possibly disappoint you! If you're shy then the idea of having a private room just for your group of people might be comforting as it takes off the pressure of singing in front of strangers as it happens in regular bars.

The rooms come with a touchscreen tablet to choose your songs from, microphones and a phone you can use to get in touch with the front desk. Most karaoke places are open 24 hours and offer food and all-you-can-drink packages delivered to your room, so if you feel like it, don't hesitate to pull an all-nighter.

25. LEARN ABOUT THE MOST TASTEFUL FORM OF JAPANESE ART

Omiya Bonsai Village dating back to 1925 is located in Saitama city, just a short train ride north from Tokyo in a quiet neighborhood consisting of several bonsai gardens and a superb art museum. The Bonsai Art Museum, however, was only added to the village in 2010 with the aim of introducing and promoting the bonsai culture.

With a collection of more than 100 bonsai, some of them preserved through generations and more than 100 years old, chances are you'll find the museum to be not only highly educative but probably among the most elegant and aesthetically pleasing establishments you've ever set foot in.

Plenty of information on growing, sculpting and caring for bonsai is provided however perhaps the most impressive section is the one on the process of appreciating bonsai. Start by imagining a great landscape compressed into a pot, then proceed to carefully examine and focus on each one of its parts, not only the overall shape and I promise you'll be fascinated!

26. HAVE AN UNFORGETTABLE ANIMAL ENCOUNTER

If you are looking to spend some quality time outdoors in the best company possible, Machida Squirrel Garden is the answer. Home to more than 200 free roaming squirrels, the place - which looks much like a backyard with many tiny wooden houses and plenty of space - is a genuine playground for the animals. While the superstars of the place are the squirrels, a variety of other small critters such as rabbits, parrots or guinea pigs call the enclosure home.

The entrance fee is a real bargain and so is the animal food (consisting of vegetables and sunflower seeds) which I would advise you to buy as it is the best approach to bond and get the animals' undivided attention.

During feeding, be careful as the squirrels' tiny claws are quite sharp and they're serious about wanting their snack. No worries though cause you'll be provided with a mitten to prevent any minor injuries. However, once fed, the squirrels turn out to be surprisingly keen on posing for the camera. The more treats you're willing to give, the more great shots you're likely to get!

Keep in mind that these pocket-sized creatures are playful and unafraid of human interaction, hence having them climb on your back or prepared to jump on your hand is common. Don't be scared though, it's all unharmful play and part of the fun!

27. MAKE A WISH AND LET IT HAPPEN

One can never run out of things to desire or hope for in the future and one Shinto custom that has become increasingly popular among travelers is the using of Ema to address hopes to Shinto gods.

Ema are small wooden plaques used by worshipers to write down prayers and wishes and left hanging on the shrine's grounds where Gods are believed to receive them.

Perhaps, the most extensive display of Ema can be found at Meiji Jingu, one of Tokyo's most visited shrines, however you might want some privacy or a bit of time to think of your heart's desires and that's why I'd suggest choosing a smaller, quieter and less crowded shine for this endeavor. For instance, my very own tablet lives on Yasukuni Jinja's grounds, a small shrine located in central Tokyo, right next to the Imperial Palace.

Ema are available for purchase directly from the shrine's attendants. Use the back of the plaque to write your personal wish on and then hang it up in the designated area hoping that kami (the enshrined deities) will be quick to grant it.

28. SIP ON DRINKS AT AN EXTRAVAGANT ART EXHIBITION

If you happen to be passing through Tokyo anytime between July and September here's an event you don't want to miss out on - the Eco Edo

Paula Danciu

Nihonbashi Art Aquarium. The event is held on a yearly basis at Nihonbashi Mitsui Hall and has become one of Tokyo's summer traditions.

This one-of-a-kind art display has as the central piece thousands of goldfish displayed in ornamental tanks of all shapes and sizes. The event setting is fairly stylish and creates a vibrant posh atmosphere. Take your time to carefully inspect the exhibits and watch the superb goldfish gracefully swimming in the crystal clear waters.

What is interesting about the concept is that it combines two key features of the Japanese culture – people's admiration for kingyo (goldfish) and traditional elements of the Edo period.

But wait as this is getting even better! Every evening from 7 pm, the Art Aquarium turns into the Night Aquarium and the venue transforms into a veritable party spot featuring a light show, house music playing in the background and sure, alcohol consumption. Treat yourself to a glass of wine, wander through the venue and mingle with fellow art lovers. If clubbing is your cup of tea, make sure to stop by on the weekend when DJs both local and international are invited to perform.

While there is no dress code, keep in mind that the exhibition is quite sophisticated and just a little bit snobbish and most people tend to dress up elegantly.

The event is held at several different locations throughout Japan, so depending on your trip dates, you might be able to catch it elsewhere if not in Tokyo.

29. GREET THE ROYALS AT THEIR OWN RESIDENCE

Consider yourself lucky if you happen to be in Tokyo on either December 23rd of January 2nd as you'll get the unmissable opportunity to see and greet the Japanese Imperial family with the occasion of the Emperor's birthday and the New Year's greeting, respectively.

Every year, on those two dates, locals gather at the Imperial Palace - the imperial residence - where the Emperor and his family are scheduled to have several public appearances on a balcony to address and wave to the audience.

Paper flags are provided at the entrance and later used by the crowd to energetically wave as the sovereign comes into sight. This powerful moment is shared by tens of thousands of people and it is impressive to witness the love and appreciation Japanese people have for the royal family.

If you cannot make it for those dates, make sure to at least stop for a refreshing stroll in the East Gardens of the palace, a gorgeous green space of such great tranquility it makes you quickly forget you're in the center of Tokyo.

30. PADDLE UNDER THE BLOSSOMING CHERRY TREES

Sakura is likely to be the most awaited season of the year, a time when families, friends and colleagues gather for hanami, the Japanese tradition of cherry blossom viewing.

Chidorigafuchi moat which encircles the Imperial Palace is one of Tokyo's most outstanding sakura spots, one that attracts heaps of visitors every spring. More than 200 trees line up along the banks of the moat making for a breathtaking landscape.

Have the best hanami experience by renting a boat from the boat pier and sail along the moat under the blooming pink branches. For a more romantic atmosphere, consider stopping by in the evening, as night illuminations are being held daily throughout the season.

31. COOK YOUR OWN JAPANESE MEAL

Your culinary journey in Tokyo cannot be concluded without an okonomiyaki meal. This cabbage based pancake-like dish literally translates from Japanese as 'grilled as you like it' and is sometimes referred to as the Japanese pizza due to its adaptability.

Countless options for fillings and toppings are available and what goes into preparing the meal will depend mainly on your own personal taste. The basic ingredients include the batter and plenty of shredded cabbage, but other than that you can go for anything from meat and seafood to cheese, noodles or rice cake.

What makes the dining experience unique is that you have the chance to cook the pancake yourself from the scratch. Nothing to be worried about though, as the restaurant staff will be more than happy to give you a helping hand in case you need it.

Tokyo is filled with restaurants that specialize in this particular dish and many of them come equipped with dining tables that have a built it iron griddle. Make sure to choose one of those eateries to get the full okonomiyaki experience.

The cooking process itself is uncomplicated and can be best enjoyed over a drink and a good conversation. The ingredients will be served in a bowl and all you need to do is thoroughly mix everything together and fry it on the hot surface. Tables come with metal spatulas used to handle the mix and later on cut the pancake into smaller portions. Once the cooking part is complete, the food remains on the griddle keeping it warm throughout the entire meal.

All that's left to do is garnishing the dish with sauces and toppings and savoring every single bite.

32. PARTY LIKE A CHAMPION

If you're thinking of a fun night out in Tokyo, Golden Gai in Shinjuku is the place to pinpoint on your map. The drinking district is packed with micro bars and eateries and attracts many tourists and locals alike.

Make sure to stop by Champion Bar for a few drinks and free karaoke. You know you've reached the bar when you come across a large group of loud people drinking outside (the place is a magnet for customers and gets crowded quickly).

The place has a great atmosphere and it's a cool spot to meet new people and experience the city's party scene. Karaoke certainly connects people so make sure to sing along.

33. BE DAZZLED AT TOKYO'S WACKIEST CAFÉ

From the country that gave the world sushi and bullet trains, now comes the Kawaii Monster extravaganza. Located in Harajuku, a district famous for its extreme fashion scene, the café is the pure embodiment of Harajuku's spirit: colorful, loud and quirky. Truth be told, this café would make sense nowhere else in Tokyo but here.

Get ready to be devoured by a (cute!) monster at the entrance as all the action takes place in its belly. With a decor including giant animal heads sucking on milk bottles hanging from the ceiling, booth seating beneath gigantic multicolored flowers and distorted mirrors, this place is eccentric to say at least.

The menu fits the pattern and includes dishes such as the colorful rainbow pasta which is served on a painter's palette of sauces or the colorful poison parfait, a multi-layered dessert.

The café is popular especially among Japanese youngsters and families with small children as well as tourists seeking a taste of Tokyo's weirdness.

The best part about this place is the overall atmosphere though. Things heat up when the so-called monster girls adorned with freakish costumes and multi-colored wigs take the stage for the hourly dance show, to which everyone is invited to participate.

The café quickly gets a jolly vibe as customers all gather around the stage and start dancing and singing together.

While a visit is something I warmly encourage you to plan, deciding whether Kawaii Monster Café is interesting or uniquely bizarre, it's all up to you!

34. GET AN ADRENALINE RUSH IN THE HEART OF TOKYO

If you're in for a dose of adrenaline, look no further than Tokyo Dome City Attractions. Located in central Tokyo, the amusement park can be enjoyed by grownups and children alike as it comes with 20+ attractions suitable for different age groups.

To make the most out of the park's attractions, the day pass is probably the best deal as it grants access to unlimited rides during the park's business hours. Depending on how much time you'd like to allocate, starting from 5 pm you can opt for the night pass at a reduced fare. A visit in the afternoon also helps avoid crowds and queues. Tickets can be bought directly at the venue from the ticket counter near the entrance.

The amusement park's pièce de résistance is the Thunder Dolphin, a rollercoaster which offers a thrilling ride that's second to none. Scary here and then, the feeling of flying between skyscrapers is worth the visit alone.

Make sure not to miss a slow ride on the Ferris Wheel as due to the park's proximity to the city center, you'll have a superb view over the Tokyo cityscape. The wheel might be moving at a snail's pace, but the ride is far from being dull as each cabin is equipped with its own entertainment system, containing music and information about various tourist spots.

Aside from the amusement park, Tokyo Dome City is known as a shopping and dining center so anytime you feel like taking a break from the rides or would like to grab something to eat or drink, head off for one of its many restaurants or cafes.

35. WALK THROUGH A WINTER WONDERLAND

Tokyo is by default dazzling and animated, however, as soon as the cold season starts - sometime around early-November - the city embraces the holiday spirit and transforms itself into a veritable winter wonderland. As part of the annual tradition, the entire city lights up, trees and buildings are decorated with millions of colorful lights and the atmosphere becomes more vivid and festive as ever.

If you happen to be in town during winter, don't hesitate to spend your evenings roaming around the city as the illuminations will warm up your heart, leave you speechless and provide memorable photo locations. Remember though that winters in Tokyo can be quite cold and windy so make sure to put on several layers before leaving the house.

If I had to choose favorites spots, I'd pick Shibuya's glowing blue cavern (check the schedule for "Ao no Dokutsu"), Yebisu Garden Place as it features a superb Christmas tree and a western style market (and there's no better way to experience the holiday vibe and fight the cold than a cup of tea or a glass of mulled wine) and Rikugien, one of Tokyo's most spectacular gardens, which is holding evening illuminations after normal opening hours.

36. VISIT THE FAKE FOOD REALM

One distinctive feature of Japanese restaurants is the window display of fake food. Most eateries use eye-catching plastic food samples to make their menus more appealing and ease the ordering process for non-Japanese speaking customers.

Fake samples are made with such precision and a high level of detail which makes them hard to tell apart from the real dishes.

The source for plastic food is Kappabashi Dougu street in Asakusa, Japan's largest shopping street specialized in kitchen equipment. Head off to this hot spot for a large display of fake Japanese specialties and while you're there make sure to purchase some „fresh" sushi to surprise your friends and family back home.

37. TIME TRAVEL FROM EDO TO TOKYO

Edo-Tokyo museum will take you through 400 years of history tracking Tokyo's (formerly known as Edo) industrial, economic and cultural evolution since its humble beginnings up until the present day.

To make the most out of the visit I'd advise you to join one of the free guided tours that are led in several languages by knowledgeable volunteers.

With an impressive collection of exhibits spread over two sections, namely the Edo Zone and the Tokyo Zone, to say this establishment is a regular museum would be an understatement. Think of it more as a theme park.

Once inside, it does not take long before feeling transported right back into the past. At the entrance, dominating the venue is a real-life replica of the Nihonbashi wooden bridge initially built in 1608 that visitors need to cross before reaching the exhibition halls.

The items on display include miniature versions of people, buildings and parts of the city, full-size models of houses visitors can have a peek in and reconstructions of daily life scenes from the Edo Period.

The exhibition is interactive as it is comprehensive and offers plenty of hands-on experience and cool photo opportunities. Make sure to take a picture with the gorgeous staging of the Kabuki theatre performance, ride an old school rickshaw and check out how a standard post-war apartment room looked like.

38. GO FOR A CITY BREAK IN YOKOHAMA

Less than an hour's train ride south from Tokyo is Yokohama, Japan's second largest city, a charming port town home to superb architecture, vibrant jazz scene and a bustling Chinatown. Yokohama makes for an excellent day trip from Tokyo and I'll suggest you start your day early as this tourist hub is more than generous when it comes to entertainment options.

A walk around the picturesque harbor is an absolute must. Go for a relaxing stroll in Yamashita Park, which stretches along the waterfront and let the refreshing breeze cool your face, then stop to take some inspiring photos of Yokohama's iconic skyline with the futuristic Minato Mirai 21 area in the background.

Food-wise, when in Yokohama, Chinese is the way to go! The colorful narrow streets of Chinatown are filled with countless restaurants and most eateries will have all-you-can-eat deals so you can feast on a wide assortment of dishes.

The city looks astonishing after dark. For the very best panoramic view, stop by the Landmark Tower and take the elevator up to the 69th floor to the Sky Garden Observatory. Let your eyes fill with marvel as the sparkling city lights create an out-of-this-world scenery.

Yokohama is also known as the home of jazz and there's no better way to chill after a full day of sightseeing than dropping by one of its many music bars for a few drinks and a live performance. If you're a fan of the genre and happen to be around in

October, check for tickets at Yokohama Jazz
Promenade, one of Japan's largest jazz festivals held
on a yearly basis.

*"Tokyo would probably be the foreign city if I had
to eat one city's food for the rest of my life, every day.
It would have to be Tokyo, and I think the majority of
chefs you ask that question would answer the same
way."*
Anthony Bourdain

39. FEAST ON A BELOVED NATIONAL DISH AT A FANTASTIC MUSEUM

Inspired by a Chinese noodle dish, ramen is today
one of Japan's culinary delights, famous for its
elaborate soup containing five up to forty ingredients
which create some truly unique flavors. In its honor,
the Shin-Yokohama Ramen Museum was founded in
1994 as the world's first food-themed amusement
park and brings together under one roof flavors from
all over Japan.

Paula Danciu

The establishment is designed as a fusion between museum and dining quarter so you can easily get your dose of ramen knowledge as well as have a ramen feast at one or more of the several shops available.

Once inside, you'll take a big step back in time, as the interior recreates an outdoor setting of Japan of the year 1958 (when the world's first instant ramen was invented) with the ceiling painted to resemble a night sky, narrow streets, clothes hanging by the window and instrumental music playing in the background.

My most precious piece of advice would be to go to the museum on an empty stomach as various types of ramen are available and it's a good idea to try out different dishes and flavors. Each shop gives the option to purchase "mini ramen" or half-size ramen bowls, however, keep in mind that these are in fact consistent bowls of food, called "mini" solely because the regular portions are gigantic.

40. EXPLORE TOKYO'S ELECTRIC TOWN

Massive buildings covered in flashy advertising, large TV screens playing loud music, young girls dressed up as French maids and electronic shops everywhere you look – this is Akihabara in a nutshell.

This vibrant district, nicknamed the Electric Town is known as the mecca of cheap electronic shops and center of otaku culture in Tokyo. Whether you're after cool gadgets, collect anime or enjoy a pulsating atmosphere, Akihabara will instantly mesmerize you.

If you happen to be in Tokyo during the weekend, consider visiting on Sunday afternoon, when the main street is closed to car traffic.

Also make sure to stop by the mega-sized Yodobashi Camera, an electronics haven, if not for shopping, for the overall experience. When you're in need of a rest, look for the store's section with the massage chairs and sample a few of them free of charge.

41. DRINK AND DINE AT A JAPANESE INSTITUTION

The Japanese have something of a love affair with izakaya and unwinding over drinks after a long day's work in the company of friends and colleagues is one of the most common features of social life in Tokyo.

Izakaya are inexpensive traditional pubs, a mix between drinking establishment and eatery where locals love to spend their evenings sharing food and chatting away over beers.

The ambiance of an izakaya is hard to match. As gathering spots for big groups of people, these places are usually loud, vivid and you'll find yourself surrounded by happy faces in a laughter-filled atmosphere.

If this is your first visit to Tokyo, an izakaya dinner is a good opportunity to be introduced to a large array of Japanese dishes. Typical ones include yakitori, karaage, grilled fish, sushi, sashimi, nabe, fries and salads. To feel like you're getting your money's worth, it's a good idea to go for an all-you-can-eat & all-you-can-drink package, keeping in mind that these deals come with a time limit that varies between one and two hours.

When deciding on a place, chain izakaya are perhaps the best option in terms of food variety, price and access. Shops are normally spread in all major districts of Tokyo and since they cater to locals and foreigners alike, English menus or menus with pictures are common.

Some chains known for their unbeatable prices and good quality food are Chiba Chan (famous for their giant and delicious karaage), Torikizoku (specialized in yakitori or chicken skewers), Isomaru suisan (ideal for fish lovers, tables come with a grill, so you can cook your own food), Hanbey (retro decor inspired by the Showa period) and Za Watami (these shops tend to be on a more quieter side having private elegant rooms available).

42. EXPERIENCE THE JAPANESE WAY OF NOMINICATION

Besides helping locals unbend their minds from work, drinking in Japan is also seen as a way of self-expression - so much so that even a new word has been invented to describe the art of expressing oneself through drinking. That word is nominication ("nomu" meaning to drink).

Many alcoholic beverages serve the purpose of nominication. Much like anywhere else in the world, beer is a widely popular choice in Tokyo. However, the most emblematic Japanese drink, renowned worldwide is Nihonshu, otherwise known as sake or rice wine. This can be drunk either cold or hot. A much stronger alternative to sake is shochu, commonly served with water and ice or fruit juices and often used as a cocktail base.

If you're not much of a drinker or the taste of strong alcohol doesn't appeal to you, go for a glass of umeshu (plum wine), a sweet, fruity liquor which tastes more like juice or a glass of highball, a carbonated drink, mix of whisky and soda, which comes with a wide range of flavors. Similar to Highball is Chuhai, a fruit-flavored shochu-based canned drink which can be bought at any shop that sells alcohol.

You can easily get these traditional drinks at any izakaya chain that I previously recommended. One other place known for its crazy cheap drinks is Medaka, a multistory izakaya located in Kabukicho, Tokyo's red-light district.

If you'd like to glam up your evening, stop by Hachigatsu no Kujira, a fancy bar in Shibuya, and have a glass of your favorite movie, as this place is famous for the novelty of creating cocktails based on film names.

When making a toast, the key word is "Kanpai!"

43. SPEND A WILD NIGHT-IN

Traveling with your significant other? Maybe yes, maybe not! This is for all those traveling with a partner yet not limited to.

Love hotels. A way more entertaining and provocative alternative for a romantic escapade to regular hotels which suddenly appear dull when competing against themed rooms, mirrored ceilings, vibrating beds and Jacuzzi tubs.

Also referred to as "leisure hotels", these are decent, clean establishments with prices comparable to those of conventional hotels and cater to anyone looking for a creative and inspiring space to spend some unwinding time with a special companion.

Love hotels in Japan serve not only as secret rendezvous for playful lovers but are familiar to many dating and married couples keen for some privacy outside of their thin-walled Japanese homes.

Tokyo has hundreds of such hotels spread all over the city. While they are easily identifiable due to kitschy façades decorated with neon colors and bright signs, when it comes to etiquette discretion is the norm! Privacy and anonymity are granted to all parties involved and face-to-face contact is almost never made with hotel staff, as they're seated behind opaque screens showing no more than a pair of floating hands.

Choosing a room feels like shopping from a catalogue. A panel of photos with the available rooms and features is normally shown at the entrance and selection is made by pressing a button. Payment is either done through a machine or directly to the pair of hands at the reception.

Depending on the amount of love one has to offer, guests can choose between a "rest" (lasting about a couple of hours) or a stay (overnight stay).

44. INDULGE IN HARAJUKU'S SIGNATURE FOOD

Craving something sweet? Head over to Harajuku to have a taste of its signature food – the crêpes. While there are many places within the area selling

79

the pancake, Takeshita-dori is unquestionably the crêpe kingdom. This 400-meter long pedestrian street has the largest concentration of shops with an astonishing variety of appetizing fillings.

The street tends to be busy at all times and gets especially crowded on weekends. Crowded as it might be, make sure to stop by one of the stalls for a delicious and inexpensive dessert and get ready to be pleasantly surprised by the creativity that goes into creating them.

The crepe might have French origins, but the Japanese took things to another level when it comes to the mix of toppings, so don't be too surprised if some crepes come with entire slices of cake chucked in the middle!

45. VISIT THE PARK THAT KEEPS ON GIVING

Whether you're a culture vulture or a nature observer, Ueno Park has the potential to deliver beyond any touristic expectations. The park is a site of major cultural, historic and religious significance and home to several museums, temples, shrines and Japan's oldest zoo.

Nature-wise, a visit to the park during certain periods of time will quickly leave you speechless. One of those times is the cherry blossom season when the 1000 cherry trees lining its central pathway create a splendid pink tunnel and the other is sometime around late July- mid August when Shinobazu, the large lotus pond, is in full bloom, its green leaves covering the pond's surface to the point where the body of water is not visible anymore.

After visiting the park more times than I can remember I can honestly say that is impossible to cover the whole area in just one day. Therefore, here are a few suggestions to consider when planning your stop:

-       pay a visit to Tokyo National Museum, Japan's oldest and largest museums, to have a look at an extensive collection of artworks and archaeological items including national treasures and important cultural properties

- spend a couple of hours strolling through Japan's first zoological garden and meet the zoo's stars - two giant pandas and one single polar bear which can be seen diving in his tank

- find some peace and quiet in the middle of the pond by renting a pedal-powered swan from the park's boat dock and spend half an hour floating around and bird watching

46. TAKE THE PULSE OF THE CITY IN A FORMER BLACK MARKET

Just across the street from Ueno Park is Ameyoko, an open-air market known for its rock-bottom prices, which used to serve as a black market for mainly sugary products in the years following WW2.

Nowadays, the market sells everything from clothes and cosmetics to fresh foods and golf gear and it's a popular destination for second-hand goods, also home to many small open-air eateries and restaurants.

Expect the typical market atmosphere: bright, colorful and extremely loud. I'd say Ameyoko becomes especially lively after dark so it's a good idea to take an evening stroll looking for bargain souvenirs to take back to your friends and family.

When you're ready for a snack, make sure to stop by Gindaco (a chain restaurant with shops located around train and metro stations) for a plate of finger-licking takoyaki, a type of street food originally from Osaka yet beloved nationwide. Takoyaki are dough balls containing octopus pieces, crispy on the outside and gooey on the inside, which come with a variety of toppings.

If you're looking for something more refreshing, don't hesitate to buy some fruits on sticks from street sellers for a price next to nothing.

47. HANG OUT AT A CAT CAFE

If the thought of being in a room full of fluffy pets makes you smile, then you must make it a priority to stop by one of Tokyo's many cat cafes. The concept is largely popular in Tokyo and first appeared in Asia in order to meet the needs of animal lovers who were not allowed to keep pets in their apartments. Things haven't changed much nowadays, hence these cafés are scattered all over the city.

If you're keen on squeezing in some playtime with the kittens in between your sightseeing activities, I'm happy to recommend Calico, a 2 story cat cafe located in Shinjuku, one of Tokyo's busiest and most entertaining districts. You'll find the place to be spacious and cozy and the pets looking clean, healthy and relaxed.

Upon entering, you'll have to pay a time-based cover charge, take off your shoes and wash your hands before getting in contact with the felines and once you do, don't be disappointed if they look unimpressed with you, as they are already familiar with visitors and know exactly how charming and lovely they are and how sought-after their attention is. They don't have any issue with having their photo taken though.

And remember, when trying to bond, cat food (available for purchase) really helps!

48. EXPERIENCE AUTHENTIC JAPANESE HOSPITALITY

Dating back to 1673, Mitsukoshi Nihonbashi is Japan's oldest department store and one of the most luxurious and prestigious shopping centers in Tokyo.

Make sure to stop by its entrance at 10 am as the store opening ceremony is something that has to be seen to be believed. The opening starts with a short speech held by one of the store clerks, welcoming customers in both Japanese and English.

Once the doors open, customers are welcomed by the employees who have already lined up in front of their shops ready for the greeting routine. You'll feel that your visit is celebrated and much appreciated as each employee will warmly greet you with a smile and a bow.

This proof of authentic Japanese hospitality will surely add up to your overall shopping experience.

Before leaving make sure to visit the food hall, located in the basement for a wide display of Japanese specialties and gorgeously wrapped sweets. Products are available for takeaway and some stalls occasionally offer free samples.

49. CRUISE AWAY IN THE BAY

Tokyo is certainly beautiful viewed from land but seen from a boat is a whole new adventure. Many companies operate cruises on Tokyo Bay and depending on your preferences and budget, you have plenty of options to choose from.

Tokyo Cruise Ship, for example, has a number of cruises connecting Asakusa and Hinode Piers to Odaiba and prides itself in its two sci-fi flagship vessels, Himiko or Hotaluna which look more like spaceships than boats. If you'd like to kill two birds with one stone consider taking the Asakusa-Hamarikyu route which sails along Sumida River, slips under several bridges and takes you to one of Tokyo's most enchanting gardens.

If you prefer a more authentic setting and delightful night views, a Yakatabune dinner cruise might be just for you. These are traditional tour boats, adorned with red lanterns on the outside and have a Japanese style interior with low tables and tatami-matted floors. This type of cruises usually last for 2 or 3 hours during which you'll enjoy traditional Japanese cuisine and beverages.

50. ATTEND A JAPANESE MATSURI

One last experience to tick off your Tokyo bucket list is partaking in a traditional Japanese festival, called matsuri. Matsuri are lively, colorful and rich in tradition and provide a great occasion to experience Tokyo's cultural scene and mingle with locals.

The city holds many festivals all year long, ranging from traditional religious parades to modern dancing festivals. Whenever you decide to visit, chances are some festivities will take place somewhere around the city. Make sure then to do a little research beforehand based on your trip dates.

Paula Danciu

Tokyo has too many festivals to fit on one list. Some of the most spectacular are Kanda Matsuri, Sanno Matsuri, Sanja Matsuri and the Asakusa Samba Carnival to name just a few.

Some other season-related events beloved by locals are hanami (cherry blossom viewing) in spring or hanabi taikai (fireworks displays) in summer.

TOP REASONS TO BOOK THIS TRIP

Fascinating culture: Japan has one of the richest and most captivating cultures in the world with centuries-old traditions that are kept alive and celebrated to this day.

Unparalleled food scene: Japanese cuisine is internationally acclaimed and Tokyo is a veritable food paradise, home to uncountable restaurants well-fitted to every taste and budget.

Mesmerizing nature: The sacred appreciation Japanese people have for Mother Nature and its boundless beauty is reflected in the pristine condition of Tokyo's many natural spaces and picture-perfect gardens.

Paula Danciu

Bonus Book

50 THINGS TO KNOW ABOUT PACKING LIGHT FOR TRAVEL

Pack the Right Way Every Time

Author: Manidipa
Bhattacharyya

Paula Danciu

Edited by Melanie Howthorne

Introduction

He who would travel happily
must travel light.

-Antoine de Saint-Exupéry

Travel takes you to different places from seas and mountains to deserts and much more. In your travels you get to interact with different people and their cultures. You will, however, enjoy the sights and interact positively with these new people even more, if you are travelling light.

When you travel light your mind can be free from worry about your belongings. You do not have to spend precious vacation time waiting for your luggage to arrive after a long flight. There is no chance of your bags going missing and the best part is that you need not pay a fee for checked baggage.

People who have mastered this art of packing light will root for you to take only one carry-on, wherever you go. However, many people can find it really hard to pack light. More so if you are travelling with children. Differentiating between "must have" and "just in case" items is the starting point. There will be ample shopping avenues at your destination which are just waiting to be explored.

Paula Danciu

This book will show you 'packing' in a new 'light' –
pun intended – and help you to embrace light
packing practices for all of your future travels.

Off to packing!

Dedication

I dedicate this book to all the travel buffs that I know,
who have given me great insights into the contents of
their backpacks.

About The Author

Manidipa Bhattacharyya is a creative writer and editor, with an education in English literature and Linguistics. After working in the IT industry for seven long years she decided to call it quits and follow her heart instead. Manidipa has been ghost writing, editing, proof reading and doing secondary research services for many story tellers and article writers for about three years. She stays in Kolkata, India with her husband and a busy two year old. In her own time Manidipa enjoys travelling, photography and writing flash fiction.

Manidipa believes in travelling light and never carries anything that she couldn't haul herself on a trip. However, travelling with her child changed the scenario. She seemed to carry the entire world with her for the baby on the first two trips. But good sense prevailed and she is again working her way to becoming a light traveler, this time with a kid.

The Right Travel Gear

1. Choose Your Travel Gear Carefully

While selecting your travel gear, pick items that are light weight, durable and most importantly, easy to carry. There are cases with wheels so you can drag them along – these are usually on the heavy side because of the trolley. Alternatively a backpack that you can carry comfortably on your back, or even a duffel bag that you can carry easily by hand or sling across your body are also great options. Whatever you choose, one thing to keep in mind is that the luggage itself should not weigh a ton, this will give you the flexibility to bring along one extra pair of shoes if you so desire.

2. Carry The Minimum Number Of Bags

Selecting light weight luggage is not everything. You need to restrict the number of bags you carry as well. One carry-on size bag is ideal for light travel. Most carriers allow one cabin baggage plus one purse, handbag or camera bag as long as it slides under the seat in front. So technically, you can carry two items of luggage without checking them in.

3. Pack One Extra Bag

Always pack one extra empty bag along with your essential items. This could be a very light weight duffel bag or even a sturdy tote bag which takes up minimal space. In the event that you end up buying a lot of souvenirs, you already have a handy bag to stuff all that into and do not have to spend time hunting for an appropriate bag.

I'm very strict with my packing and have everything in its right place. I never change a rule. I hardly use anything in the hotel room. I wheel my own wardrobe in and that's it.

Charlie Watts

Clothes & Accessories

4. Plan Ahead

Figure out in advance what you plan to do on your trip. That will help you to pick that one dress you need for the occasion. If you are going to attend a wedding then you have to carry formal wear. If not, you can ditch the gown for something lighter that will be comfortable during long walks or on the beach.

5. Wear That Jacket

Remember that wearing items will not add extra luggage for your air travel. So wear that bulky jacket that you plan to carry for your trip. This saves space and can also help keep you warm during the chilly flight.

6. Mix and Match

Carry clothes that can be interchangeably used to reinvent your look. Find one top that goes well with a couple of pairs of pants or skirts. Use tops, shirts and jackets wisely along with other accessories like a scarf or a stole to create a new look.

7. Choose Your Fabric Wisely

Stuffing clothes in cramped bags definitely takes its toll which results in wrinkles. It is best to carry wrinkle free, synthetic clothes or merino tops. This will eliminate the need for that small iron you usually bring along.

8. Ditch Clothes, Pack Underwear

Pack more underwear and socks. These are the things that will give you a fresh feel even if you do not get a chance to wear fresh clothes. Moreover these are easy to wash and can be dried inside the hotel room itself.

9. Choose Dark Over Light

While picking your clothes, choose dark coloured ones. They are easy to colour coordinate and can last longer before needing a wash. Accidental food spills and dirt from the road are less visible on darker clothes.

10. Wear Your Jeans

Take only one pair of jeans with you, which you should wear on the flight. Remember to pick a pair that can be worn for sightseeing trips and is equally eloquent for dinner. You can add variety by adding light weight cargoes and chinos.

11. Carry Smart Accessories

The right accessory can give you a fresh look even with the same old dress. An intelligent neck-piece, a couple of bright scarves, stoles or a sarong can be used in a number of ways to add variety to your clothing. These light weight beauties can double up as a nursing cover, a light blanket, beach wear, a modesty cover for visiting places of worship, and also makes for an enthralling game of peek-a-boo.

12. Learn To Fold Your Garments

Seasoned travelers all swear by rolling their clothes for compact and wrinkle free packing. Bundle packing, where you roll the clothes around a central object as if tying it up, is also a popular method of compact and wrinkle free packing. Stacking folded clothes one on top of another is a big no-no as it makes creases extreme and they are difficult to get rid of without ironing.

13. Wash Your Dirty Laundry

One of the ways to avoid carrying loads of clothes is to wash the clothes you carry. At some places you might get to use the laundry services or a Laundromat but if you are in a pinch, best solution is to wash them yourself. If that is the plan then carrying quick drying clothes is highly recommended, which most often also happen to be the wrinkle free variety.

14. Leave Those Towels Behind

Regular towels take up a lot of space, are heavy and take ages to dry out. If you are staying at hotels they will provide you with towels anyway. If you are travelling to a remote place, where the availability of towels looks doubtful, carry a light weight travel towel of viscose material to do the job.

15. Use A Compression Bag

Compression bags are getting lots of recommendation nowadays from regular travelers. These are useful for saving space in your luggage when you have to pack bulky dresses. While packing for the return trip, get help from the hotel staff to arrange a vacuum cleaner.

Footwear

16. Put On Your Hiking Boots

If you have plans to go hiking or trekking during your trip, you will need those bulky hiking boots. The best way to carry them is to wear them on flight to save space and luggage weight. You can remove the boots once inside and be comfortable in your socks.

17. Picking The Right Shoes

Shoes are often the bulkiest items, along with being the dainty if you are a female. They need care and take up a lot of space in your luggage. It is advisable therefore to pick shoes very carefully. If you plan to do a lot of walking and sightseeing, then wearing a pair of comfortable walking shoes are a must. For more formal occasions you can carry durable, light weight flats which will not take up much space.

18. Stuff Shoes

If you happen to pack a pair of shoes, ensure you utilize their hollow insides. Tuck small items like rolled up socks or belts to save space. They will also be easy to find.

Toiletries
19. Stashing Toiletries

Carry only absolute necessities. Airline rules dictate that for one carry-on bag, liquids and gels must be in 3.4 ounce (100ml) bottles or less, and must be packed in a one quart zip-lock bag. If you are planning to stay in a hotel, the basic things will be provided for you. It's best to buy the rest from the local market at your destination.

20. Take Along Tampons

Tampons are a hard to find item in a lot of countries. Figure out how many you need and pack accordingly. For longer stays you can buy them online and have them delivered to where you are staying.

21. Get Pampered Before You Travel

Some avid travelers suggest getting a pedicure and manicure just the day before travelling. This not only gives you a well kept look, but also saves you the trouble of packing nail polish. Remember, every little bit of weight reduced adds up.

Electronics
22. Lugging Along Electronics

Electronics have a large role to play in our lives today. Most of us cannot imagine our lives away from our phones, laptops or tablets. However while travelling, one must consider the amount of weight these electronics add to our luggage. Thankfully smart phones come along with all the essentials tools like a camera, email access, picture editing tools and more. They are smart to the point of eliminating the need to carry multiple gadgets. Choose a smart phone that suits all your requirements and travel with the world in your palms or pocket.

23. Reduce the Number of Chargers

If you do travel with multiple electronic devices, you will have to bear the additional burden of carrying all their chargers too. Check if a single charger can be used for multiple devices. You might also consider investing in a pocket charger. These small devices support multiple gadgets while keeping you charged on the go.

24. Travel Friendly Apps

Along with smart phones come numerous apps, which are immensely helpful in our travels. You name it and you have an app for it at hand – take pictures, sharing with friends and family, torch to light dark roads, maps, checking flight/train times, find hotels and many other things. Use these smart alternatives to traditional items like books to eliminate weight and save space.

I get ideas about what's essential when packing my suitcase.

-Diane von Furstenberg

Travelling With Kids

25. Bring Along the Stroller

Kids might enjoy walking for a while but they soon tire out and a stroller is the just the right thing for them to rest in while you continue your tour. Strollers also double duty as a luggage carrier and shopping bag holder. Remember to pick a light weight, easy to handle brand of stroller. Better yet, find out in advance if you can rent a stroller at your destination.

26. Bring Only Enough Diapers for Your Trip

Diapers take up a lot of space and add to the weight of your luggage. Therefore it is advisable to carry just enough diapers to last through the trip and a few for afterwards, till you buy fresh stock at your destination. Unless of course you are travelling to a really remote area, in which case you have no choice but to carry the load. Otherwise diapers are something you will find pretty easily.

27. Take Only A Couple Of Toys

Children are easily attracted by new things in their environment. While travelling they will find numerous 'new' objects to scrutinize and play with. Packing just one favorite toy is enough, or if there is no favorite toy leave out all of them in favor of stories or imaginary games.

28. Carry Kid Friendly Snacks

Create a small snack counter in your bag to store away quick bites for those sudden hunger pangs. Depending on the child's age this could include chocolates, raisins, dry fruits, granola bars or biscuits. Also keep a bottle of water handy for your little one. These things do not add much weight and can be adjusted in a handbag or knapsack.

29. Games to Carry

Create some travel specific, imaginary games if you have slightly grown up children, like spot the attractions. Keep a coloring book and colors handy for in-flight or hotel time. Apps on your smart phone can keep the children engaged with cartoons and story books. Older children are often entertained by games available on phones or tablets. This cuts down the weight of luggage while keeping the kids entertained.

30. Let the Kids Carry Their Load

A good thing is to start early sharing of responsibilities. Let your child pick a bag of his or her choice and pack it themselves. Keep tabs on what they are stuffing in their bags by asking if they will be using that item on the trip. It could start out being just an entertainment bag initially but with growing years they will learn to sort the useful from the superfluous. Children as little as four can maneuver a small trolley suitcase like a pro- their experience in pull along toys credit. If you are worried that you may be pulling it for them, you may want to start with a backpack.

31. Decide on Location for Children to Sleep

While on a trip you might not always get a crib at your destination, and carrying one will make life all the more difficult. Instead, call ahead to see if there are any cribs or roll out beds for children. You may even put blankets on the floor. Weave them a story about camping and they will gladly sleep without any trouble.

32. Get Baby Products Delivered At Your Destination

If you are absolutely paranoid about not getting your favorite variety of diapers or brand of baby food, check out online stores like amazon.com for services in your destination city. You can buy things online ahead of your travel and get them delivered to your hotel upon arrival.

33. Feeding Needs Of Your Infants

If you are travelling with a breastfed infant, you save the trouble of carrying bottles and bottle sanitization kits. For special food, or medications, you may need to call ahead to make sure you have a refrigerator where you are staying.

34. Feeding Needs of Your Toddler

With the progression from infancy to toddler, their dietary requirements too evolve. You will have to pack some snacks for travelling time. Fresh fruits and vegetables can be purchased at your destination. Most of the cities you travel to in whichever part of the world, will have baby food products and formulas, available at the local drug-store or the supermarket.

35. Picking Clothes for Your Baby

Contrary to popular belief, babies can do without many changes of clothes. At the most, pack 2 outfits per day. Pack mix and match type clothes for your little one as well. Pick things which are comfortable to wear and quick to dry.

36. Selecting Shoes for Your Baby

Like outfits, kids can make do with two pairs of comfortable shoes. If you can get some water resistant shoes it will be best. To expedite drying wet shoes, you can stuff newspaper in them then wrap them with newspaper and leave them to dry overnight.

37. Keep One Change of Clothes Handy

Travelling with kids can be tricky. Keep a change of clothes for the kids and mum handy in your purse or tote bag. This takes a bit of space in your hand luggage but comes extremely handy in case there are any accidents or spills.

38. Leave Behind Baby Accessories

Baby accessories like their bed, bath tub, car seat, crib etc. should be left at home. Many hotels provide a crib on request, while car seats can be borrowed from friends or rented. Babies can be given a bath in the hotel sink or even in the adult bath tub with a little bit of water. If you bring a few bath toys, they can be used in the bath, pool, and out of water. They can also be sanitized easily in the sink.

39. Carry a Small Load Of Plastic Bags

With children around, there are chances of a number of soiled clothes and diapers. These plastic bags help to sort the dirt from the clean inside your big bag. These are very light weight and come in handy to other carry stuff as well at times.

Pack with a Purpose

40. Packing for Business Trips

One neutral-colored suit should suffice. It can be paired with different shirts, ties and accessories for different occasions. One pair of black suit pants could be worn with a matching jacket for the office or with a snazzy top for dinner.

41. Packing for A Cruise

Most cruises have formal dinners, and that formal dress usually takes up a lot of space. However you might find a tuxedo to rent. For women, a short black dress with multiple accessory options will do the trick.

42. Packing for A Long Trip Over Different Climates

The secret packing mantra for travel over multiple climates is layering. Layering traps air around your body creating insulation against the cold. The same light t-shirt that is comfortable in a warmer climate can be the innermost layer in a colder climate.

Reduce Some More Weight

43. Leave Precious Things At Home

Leave at home things that you would hate to lose or get damaged. Precious jewelry, expensive gadgets or dresses, could be anything. You will not require these on your trip. Leave them at home and spare the load on your mind.

44. Send Souvenirs by Mail

If you have spent all your money on purchasing souvenirs, carrying them back in the same bag that you brought along would be difficult. Either pack everything in another bag and check it in the airport or get everything shipped to your home. Use an international carrier for a secure transit, but this could be more expensive than the checking fees at the airport.

45. Avoid Carrying Books

Books equal to weight. There are many reading apps which you can download on your smart phone or tab. Plus there are gadgets like Kindle and Nook that are thinner and lighter alternatives to your regular book.

Check, Get, Set, Check Again

46. Strategize Before Packing

Create a travel list and prepare all that you think you need to carry along. Keep everything on your bed or floor before packing and then think through once again – do I really need that? Any item that meets this question can be avoided. Remove whatever you don't really need and pack the rest.

47. Test Your Luggage

Once you have fully packed for the trip take a test trip with your luggage. Take your bags and go to town for window shopping for an hour. If you enjoy your hour long trip it is good to go, if not, go home and reduce the load some more. Repeat this test till you hit the right weight.

48. Add a Roll Of Duct Tape

You might wonder why, when this book has been talking about reducing stuff, we're suddenly asking you to pack something totally unusual. This is because when you have limited supplies, duct tape is immensely helpful for small repairs – a broken bag, leaking zip-lock bag, broken sunglasses, you name it and duct tape can fix it, temporarily.

49. List of Essential Items

Even though the emphasis is on packing light, there are things which have to be carried for any trip. Here is our list of essentials:

• Passport/Visa or any other ID

Paula Danciu

- Any other paper work that might be required on a trip like permits, hotel reservation confirmations etc.

- Medicines – all your prescription medicines and emergency kit, especially if you are travelling with children

- Medical or vaccination records

- Money in foreign currency if travelling to a different country

- Tickets- Email or Message them to your phone

50. Make the Most of Your Trip

Wherever you are going, whatever you hope to do we encourage you to embrace it whole-heartedly. Take in the scenery, the culture and above all, enjoy your time away from home.

On a long journey even a straw weighs heavy.

-Spanish Proverb

>TOURIST

Paula Danciu

Packing and Planning Tips

A Week before Leaving

- Arrange for someone to take care of pets and water plants

- Stop mail and newspaper

- Notify Credit Card companies where you are going

- Change your thermostat settings

- Car is inspected, oil is changed, and tires have the correct pressure

- Passport and id are up to date

- Pay bills

- Copy important items and download travel apps

- Start collecting small bills for tips

Right Before Leaving

- Clean out refrigerator

- Empty garbage cans

- Lock windows

- Make sure you have the right ID with you

- Bring cash for tips

- Remember travel documents

- Lock door behind you

- Remember wallet

- Unplug items in the house and pack chargers

Paula Danciu

Read other
Greater Than a Tourist
Books

Greater Than a Tourist San Miguel de Allende Guanajuato Mexico:
50 Travel Tips from a Local by Tom Peterson

Greater Than a Tourist – Lake George Area New York USA:
 50 Travel Tips from a Local by Janine Hirschklau

Greater Than a Tourist – Monterey California United States:
50 Travel Tips from a Local by Katie Begley

 Greater Than a Tourist – Chanai Crete Greece:
50 Travel Tips from a Local by Dimitra Papagrigoraki

Greater Than a Tourist – The Garden Route Western Cape Province
South Africa:
50 Travel Tips from a Local by Li-Anne McGregor van Aardt

Greater Than a Tourist – Sevilla Andalusia Spain:
50 Travel Tips from a Local by Gabi Gazon

Greater Than a Tourist – Kota Bharu Kelantan Malaysia:
50 Travel Tips from a Local by Aditi Shukla

Children's Book: Charlie the Cavalier Travels the World by Lisa
Rusczyk

Paula Danciu

> TOURIST

Visit Greater Than a Tourist for Free Travel Tips
http://GreaterThanATourist.com

Sign up for the Greater Than a Tourist Newsletter for discount days, new books, and travel information:
http://eepurl.com/cxspyf

Follow us on Facebook for tips, images, and ideas:
https://www.facebook.com/GreaterThanATourist

Follow us on Pinterest for travel tips and ideas:
http://pinterest.com/GreaterThanATourist

Follow us on Instagram for beautiful travel images:
http://Instagram.com/GreaterThanATourist

Paula Danciu

> TOURIST

Please leave your honest review of this book on Amazon and Goodreads. Please send your feedback to GreaterThanaTourist@gmail.com as we continue to improve the series. Thank you. We appreciate your positive and constructive feedback. Thank you.

Paula Danciu

NOTES

Printed in Great Britain
by Amazon